SISK  S

D0426015

Contemporary African Americans

BARBARA JORDAN

BY
DIANE PATRICK-WEXLER

RSVP
RAINTREE
STECK-VAUGHN
P U B L I S H E R S
The Steck-Vaughn Company

Austin, Texas

SISKIYOU CO. SUPT. SCHOOLS
LIBRARY
609 S. GOLD ST.
YREKA, CA 96097

Copyright © 1996, Steck-Vaughn Company. All rights reserved. No part of this book may be reproduced or utilized in any form or by any means, electronic or mechanical, including photocopying, recording, or by any information storage and retrieval system, without permission in writing from the copyright owner. Requests for permission to make copies of any part of the work should be mailed to: Copyright Permissions, Steck-Vaughn Company, P.O. Box 26015, Austin, Texas 78755. Printed in the United States of America.

Published by Raintree Steck-Vaughn, an imprint of Steck-Vaughn Company.
Produced by Mega-Books, Inc.
Design and Art Direction by Michaelis/Carpelis Design Associates.
Cover photo:©Bernard Gotfryd/Woodfin Camp & Associates.

Library of Congress Cataloging-in-Publication Data
Patrick-Wexler, Diane.
  Barbara Jordan / Diane Patrick-Wexler.
    p. cm. — (Contemporary African Americans)
  Includes index.
  ISBN 0-8172-3976-6 (Hardcover)
  ISBN 0-8114-9794-1 (Softcover)
    1. Jordan, Barbara. 1936-   —Juvenile literature.
  2. Legislators—United States—Biography—Juvenile literature.
  3. Afro-American legislators—Biography—Juvenile literature.
  4. United States. Congress. House—Biography—Juvenile literature.
  I. Title. II. Series.
  E840.8.J62P38 1996
  328.73'092—dc20   96-12611
  [B]   CIP
                                               AC
Printed and bound in the United States.

1 2 3 4 5 6 7 8 9 LB 99 98 97 96 95

Photo credits: UPI/Bettmann: pp. 4, 25, 26, 34, 36, 41; Reuters/Bettmann: p.7;*Houston Chronicle*: p. 9; Courtesy of Barbara Jordan: pp. 11, 12, 15, 16;The Bettmann Archive: p19; Barbara Jordan Archives, Texas Southern University, Houston Texas: pp. 20, 22, 30, 33; AP/Wide World Photos: pp. 29, 38, 42; Clayton Adams/Hobart and William Smith Colleges: p. 45.

Contents

As a lawyer, an elected official, and a public speaker, Barbara Jordan has had a life full of victories. She has also won many gains for poor and minority citizens. Here, Barbara Jordan celebrates her first election victory, in the 1966 race for the Texas State Senate.

Chapter **One**

"A VOICE SO POWERFUL..."

What do you do if you are not happy with the way things are? You can complain . . . or you can work to make things better.

Barbara Jordan is an African-American woman who has always wanted things to be better for African Americans and for all United States citizens. Instead of just complaining about how things were, she thought about what she could do to make things better. Soon she found an answer: She could work to make new laws. Laws, she saw, were what made people's lives either harder or easier.

So after much hard work, Barbara Jordan became an elected official who helped to make laws. These officials are elected by people who live in the same area they do. They represent, or speak for, the people who elected them. Barbara Jordan spoke for her people for many years.

Today, Barbara Jordan is retired from political

office, but, while she served, she did and said many very important things. This is why she is now one of the most admired women in the United States.

Barbara Jordan grew up in America at a time when racial segregation, or separation by skin color, was legal. This was especially true in southern states, where it was against the law for blacks and whites to use the same public areas. Signs reading "White" and "Colored" marked the separate bathrooms and water fountains in bus and train stations. (African Americans were often called "Colored" in those days.) Black people could not go into white-owned motels and restaurants, or even to white schools and churches.

As a state senator, and later as a congresswoman, Barbara Jordan helped make laws that improved the lives of African Americans and many other Americans. People have often used the words "first" and "only" when talking about Barbara Jordan. She was the first African-American woman elected to the Texas State **Senate**. She was also the first African-American woman from the South elected to the United States **Congress**.

Part of Barbara Jordan's fame comes from the powerful way she speaks. Barbara is from a family of preachers, singers, teachers, and business people. All of these people used their minds and voices to communicate. So, of course, Barbara herself became a person of words. She sang in the choir and became a debater, a public speaker, a lawyer, and a politician.

Barbara is known for her great speeches. The crowd cheers her on after a speech at the 1992 Democratic National Convention.

This respected leader has always been able to capture people's attention. With her deep voice, she speaks every word clearly, carefully, and firmly. She has a great mind and always shares her ideas so that people will understand. She also has a great sense of humor. This is why Barbara Jordan is considered one of the best living orators. When Barbara enters the room, everyone gets ready to listen.

When Barbara speaks, said Congressman William L. Clay, people "hear a voice so powerful, so awesome… that it cannot be ignored and will not be silenced."

GROWING UP IN TEXAS

Barbara Charline Jordan was born in Houston, Texas, on February 21, 1936. Like many children at the time, Barbara was not born in a hospital. She was born in her parents' home, and she was delivered by a very special person, Dr. Thelma Patten. Dr. Patten was the first African-American woman doctor in Houston. She was also family. Barbara's grandfather was the doctor's cousin. So the very first hands to touch Barbara held strong family ties to education and hard work.

There were many other ties like this in Barbara Jordan's family. Her mother, Arlyne Patten Jordan, was a highly respected orator in the local Baptist church. When Mrs. Jordan spoke, everyone listened. To get ideas for her speeches, she read a lot of books. Then she rewrote the ideas she got from the books in her own words.

Benjamin Meredith Jordan was Barbara's father. He had attended Tuskegee Institute, a well-known African-

American college in Alabama. When his mother became ill, Ben Jordan left Tuskegee and returned home to Houston. He found a job at a warehouse and joined the nearby Good Hope Missionary Baptist Church. That is where he met Arlyne Patten.

Soon after Ben returned to Houston, his mother died. Later, Ben's father married again. His new wife was named Alice Reed, but everyone called her "Gar." Gar, too, had a strong education. She was a high school English teacher.

On June 18, 1931, Ben Jordan married Arlyne Patten. Within five years, three girls were born to the

Barbara Jordan would grow up to make her parents, Arlyne and Benjamin Jordan, very proud.

Jordans. Rose Mary was the first, Bennie Meredith came next, and Barbara came last. Her middle name, Charline, was in honor of her grandfather Charles Jordan. All the girls grew to be very tall.

When Barbara was a girl, the Jordan family lived in a brick house on Sharon Street with Grandfather Jordan and Gar. The house was in a beautiful neighborhood with flowering trees in all the yards. At first, there were only two bedrooms. The three girls all slept in one little bed until Barbara's father later built a third bedroom.

When Barbara wrote her life story many years later, she described what life was like in the house on Sharon Street. Although it was crowded, the house was always full of laughter, conversation, music, and the smell of good food. The Jordan family often sang gospel tunes and played the piano together. There was no television in those days. But sometimes when Barbara came home from school, she listened to the radio with her mother. When Gar came home from teaching, she would tell about her day, sharing stories of the events at school.

In this house filled with music and song, the Jordan girls became very good singers. Rose Mary sang first soprano, and Bennie sang second soprano. Barbara, with her deep voice, sang alto. The three decided it would be fun to start a singing group. So the "Jordan Sisters" began giving concerts at their church. The girls got help from their Aunt Mamie (Gar's daughter, Mamie

Barbara (center) was the youngest of three Jordan sisters. Bennie is on the left, and Rose Mary on the right.

Reed). She gave them voice lessons. Mamie taught them the importance of speaking and singing a song correctly. She told the girls that they should use their voices to "paint a picture" for their audience. The Jordan Sisters sang throughout their high school years.

Although all the girls were close to their mother, Rose Mary was their father's favorite. He was happy that she taught Bible school at their church. Barbara and her other sister Bennie were very close to each other. Sometimes they were even mistaken for twins!

Barbara's father, Ben, was very loving toward all his daughters, but he was also very strict. He expected the girls to get only As in school. He expected them all

John Ed Patten taught his granddaughter, Barbara Jordan, to always be herself.

to go to college after high school, because he had done so. He allowed no movies, no dancing, no drinking, no smoking, and no playing cards. The girls could not even visit other people's houses!

Barbara often questioned her father's rules and ideas. Even as a young girl Barbara knew that she was not like everyone else. She had friends her own age and did things the other kids did, but she always wanted more. If Barbara did not like something, she spoke up about it. If she wanted something, she would ask for it.

On Sunday mornings, the girls went to Sunday school, then met the adults at church. The Jordans did not have much money. In spite of this, Barbara's father and Grandfather Jordan dressed up for church in neat black suits. Barbara's mother always made sure that she and the girls were beautifully dressed, with nice hats and bags, especially at Easter.

Church was very important to the Jordan family. In fact, Barbara's father became the minister at the Good Hope Missionary Baptist Church. He also sang in the choir. Sometimes Barbara would recite poems at the church. People liked her strong, clear voice. She pronounced each word carefully and properly, so that the whole audience could understand. After church, the family went to have Sunday dinner at the house of Grandfather Patten. In the afternoon the girls would have to return to the church. The problem was, Barbara really did not want to go back. That is where Grandfather Patten came in.

John Ed Patten was Arlyne Jordan's father. He adored his granddaughter Barbara from the moment she was born. He always carried a photo of her marked, "MY HEART."

Grandfather Patten had had a hard life. Years before, he had mistakenly shot a white police officer in what he thought was a robbery attempt at his candy store. He was sent to jail. Before he was pardoned by the governor, John Ed Patten served part of a ten-year prison sentence. Life with his family was a great reward after being in prison.

No one was as important to Barbara as Grandfather Patten. In her life story, Barbara writes that she loved him because he was different from the rest of the family. Like Barbara, Grandfather Patten questioned the rules. He did what he believed was right for him and did not care what other people thought about it.

Grandfather Patten was the only family member who did not attend church. One Sunday afternoon Barbara announced that she did not want to go back to church. Her Grandfather Patten simply said, "You don't have to." From then on she stayed home on Sunday afternoons to be with him. The pair always had a great time. They spent hours talking and eating barbecued ribs. Grandfather Patten talked with Barbara as if she were a grownup. He taught her important lessons about life.

Grandfather Patten shared with Barbara his love for reading. From the time Barbara was five years old, Grandfather Patten would put on his eyeglasses and read to his granddaughter from the Bible, the dictionary, and from books of poetry. He also talked to Barbara about his own family. He was very proud of his father, who was a lawyer in Washington. Barbara did not know what being a lawyer meant, but she liked how important it sounded.

Barbara learned more from Grandfather Patten than just a love for reading. He also taught her about his junk business. Grandfather Patten believed that the best thing a person could do was to be his or her own boss. He ran his own business, collecting junk from people and then selling it to others who needed it.

Barbara learned a lot by helping Grandfather Patten with his junk business. The junk was picked up in this cart, pulled by mules.

With a wagon pulled by a pair of mules, he traveled through Houston collecting things people left out for him. He loaded the goods into the wagon and brought them back home. There he sorted out the rags, paper, and metal, and sold them. He even sold manure for fertilizer.

Rose Mary and Bennie thought working with junk was below them. They would not go near it. Barbara was different. Because she loved her grandfather so much, she also loved helping him. She put on her old clothes and helped Grandfather Patten stack and tie the papers. She helped put the manure in baskets, and the rags in neat bundles.

By the age of ten, Barbara Jordan had already begun to stand up for her own ideas.

Grandfather Patten also put Barbara in charge of weighing the rags.

Dirty or not, this was a successful business. Grandfather Patten shared whatever money he made with Barbara. While her sisters looked down on the junk, Barbara was busy earning money. She was in business! This is why Barbara always had more money than her sisters. She was very proud of the way her grandfather worked hard to make a living. It did not matter what other people thought. Barbara admired her grandfather a great deal.

Grandfather Patten admired Barbara, too. He did not want her to be like other kids. He wanted her to be herself. He said, "You just trot your own horse and don't get into the same rut as everyone else." Barbara Jordan vowed she would follow his advice.

Three

LOVING TO LEARN

During Barbara's school years, it was still illegal in the South for blacks and whites to go to school together. So Barbara attended all-black schools.

Barbara was a top student in elementary school and at Phillis Wheatley High School. This school was named for the slave who became a famous poet. Barbara did the usual things that many high school girls did. She had a lot of friends, cheered the football team, and wore the latest clothes and jewelry. In her yearbook, she listed her favorite things: "EATS AND TREATS: Ice Cream... Fried Chicken;... FAVORITE MAGAZINE: Seventeen; FAVORITE DEEJAY: Dr. Daddy-O;... FASHION FADS: The poodle cut and loud-colored shoes." After school, she led her gang of friends home, laughing and talking. Sometimes it took them over an hour just to walk a few blocks!

As Barbara got older, she began to notice things that bothered her. When she went downtown, she saw the water fountains marked "White" and "Colored." She noticed the separate restrooms. She knew that lunch counters in the five-and-dime stores did not serve African Americans at all. In those days, most people did not openly question racial segregation. But Barbara Jordan hoped that some day, she would help to change things.

In the Jordan family, it was understood that everyone would go to college. Barbara realized that if she wanted to be good college material, she would have to take school extra seriously. She decided that she would have to learn to lead, instead of follow, the other students. Barbara wanted to be "Girl of the Year," the senior girl who was voted the most outstanding student. To increase her chances of winning, Barbara got involved in more school activities. She began tutoring fellow classmates. She joined school clubs, and she became president of the Honor Society.

When all her friends began to plan for their careers, most of them said they wanted to be teachers. But one day Barbara heard a woman attorney, or lawyer, speak at her high school. Barbara decided then that she was going to be a lawyer, too.

That year Barbara also became involved in speechmaking at Wheatley High School. It had always been easy for her to memorize and recite passages from books. She had done that in church and at home all her life. Barbara's school speeches impressed other students and her teachers. It was not long before teachers were suggesting that Barbara take part in debates. These are contests in which people argue two sides of an important issue. Barbara agreed to join Wheatley's debating team.

As a part of the team, Barbara won many medals for her speechmaking. But that was not the best part of her senior year in high school. The best part was that she was selected as the 1952 Girl of the Year!

That year Barbara graduated with honors from Wheatley High School. She was sixteen years old. Her debate coach suggested that she enter a state debating contest. Barbara entered and won first prize! The prize was a trip to Chicago to participate in the national

Segregation meant that blacks and whites had to use separate restaurants, bathrooms, and even water fountains.

Barbara's skills as a public speaker helped win many victories for the Texas Southern University Debate Team.

contest. This would be her first trip on a train and her first time away from home.

In Chicago, Barbara won the national contest, too. The prize was a $200 scholarship to the college of her choice. In her high school yearbook, Barbara later wrote, "My trip to Chicago was the most Wonderful, Enjoyable, Exciting, Adventurous, Adorable, Unforgettable, Rapturous—it was just the best doggone trip I have ever had!"

In the fall of 1952, Barbara Jordan enrolled at Texas

Southern University, an all-black college. Still wanting to be a lawyer, she studied political science and history. She also still wanted to stand out from other people. So Barbara did what she was best at: She joined the debating team. This is where she got the first item on her list of "firsts" and "onlys." She was the first woman to travel with Texas Southern University's Debate Team.

The debating team traveled all over the country, participating in competitions. It was on these trips that Barbara became even more aware of racism in America. Her debating team had to bring food with them so they would not have to search for restaurants that served African Americans. They also had to mark their map with the African-American motels. However, Barbara noticed that when they arrived in northern cities, she and the team could relax a little. Barbara liked that feeling of freedom. It was the first time she realized that things were a little different in places outside of the South.

Barbara graduated from Texas Southern University in 1956. Remembering her travels in the North, she decided to go to law school there. Barbara enrolled in Boston University Law School, one of two African-American women in a class of six hundred students.

At first, law school was difficult for Barbara. The professors moved quickly through the course. Students had to work hard to keep up. There was only one big exam, given at the end of the year. Hardest of

Barbara Jordan remained a top student through high school, college, and law school.

all, it seemed to Barbara that every student's father was a lawyer. She felt as if everyone else grew up knowing about the law.

After her first year's final exam, Barbara was convinced she had failed. In fact, she had passed—with above-average grades! Still, Barbara realized that to do well in law school, she would have to study harder and longer than anyone else. She put her whole mind and heart into it. In 1959, she graduated from Boston University Law School. Once again, Barbara Jordan stood out with pride. She was a lawyer!

Chapter Four

MAKING CHANGES BY MAKING LAWS

At first Barbara planned to stay in Boston after she got her law degree. An insurance company offered Barbara a job as a lawyer. She would be one of hundreds of lawyers in the company. Barbara decided she did not want to sit in a little cubbyhole and work at a dull job like this. She turned the position down.

Attorney Jordan thought about what to do next. She realized she might get more support in her new career back in Texas. More people knew her there. So Barbara returned home to Houston. The new lawyer had some business cards printed. She gave them out at church and to anyone who was interested. When people called her needing legal work, Barbara did it.

At first, her "office" was in the dining room at her parents' home. The following summer, Barbara got a job teaching at Tuskegee Institute in Alabama. When she returned home in the fall, she used her savings to rent an office.

By then it was 1960. Many important events were happening across the country. The Civil Rights Movement was beginning to make headlines. Led by Martin Luther King, Jr., and other activists, huge numbers of African Americans came together to fight for equal rights. They began to challenge segregation through nonviolent protests. They were often attacked by white racists who refused to accept the idea of change. At least six people lost their lives in events that were related to the protests.

African Americans also used the court system to fight segregation. One famous case was *Brown v. Board of Education*. This was the 1954 case which decided that segregated public schools were **unconstitutional**. In spite of the case, however, very few public schools in the South had integrated whites and blacks.

Barbara Jordan thought change was happening too slowly. She asked herself, "What can I do to help?" After thinking about it carefully, Barbara realized something. "The only way to move things along is to get in a position where you can make the laws." In the southern states, the law allowed African Americans to be treated unfairly. Barbara knew this was not right. But where were the black people in the law-making process? If African Americans had more say in making the laws, Barbara thought, then the laws would not treat them unfairly.

Making laws against racial discrimination was the

To end segregation, Dr. Martin Luther King, Jr., (front row, third from left) led nonviolent protests like this 1963 March on Washington.

key. Racial discrimination means treating people differently because of their race. To help get rid of discrimination, Barbara knew she would have to get into politics. This was a new area for her, but Barbara was not afraid to try something new.

In 1960 the people were going to elect a new President. There are two main parties, or political groups, in the United States: the Republicans and the Democrats. Each party selects people to run for office in national and state elections. That year Massachusetts Senator John F. Kennedy was running for President as a Democrat. Kennedy had shown that he cared about civil rights issues. Barbara liked what he had to say. She went to the Harris County Democratic Headquarters in Houston and volunteered to help in Kennedy's campaign.

Barbara's assignment was to get African-American voters to come out and vote Democratic. Some states in the South made it very hard for African Americans to vote. They gave tests that people had to pass before they could vote and charged a "poll tax," a fee that voters had to pay. But Barbara worked hard to encourage African Americans to vote for Kennedy. She volunteered for many jobs at the Democratic

Barbara Jordan worked on one of many programs that encouraged black people to register and vote. Here, African Americans line up to vote in a small southern town.

Headquarters. She licked stamps, addressed envelopes, and even swept floors. She also traveled to churches and schools to explain the voter program.

One night, the usual speechmaker could not attend, so Barbara filled in. Barbara's powerful words captured the audience's attention. From then on, it was Barbara who made the speeches for the Harris County Democrats. Whenever a group needed a speaker, Barbara would go. Her name started appearing in the newspapers. This young African-American woman's skills as a lawyer and a speaker began to bring her a great deal of attention.

Barbara's efforts helped make the voter program Harris County's most successful ever. Most black voters did come out and vote. Kennedy and his vice president, Lyndon B. Johnson, won the election. The experience taught Barbara that she really loved political work. A coworker suggested that Barbara run for the Texas **House of Representatives** in the 1962 election. If she won, Barbara would help to make laws for the state of Texas. Barbara liked that idea. This was Barbara Jordan's chance to become a lawmaker—just what she wanted! Barbara studied the way Texas state government worked. Then she started on her political campaign.

Barbara made many speeches in her campaign for the Texas House of Representatives. She talked about what new laws needed to be made. She talked about what old laws needed to be changed. She listened to the concerns and complaints of the voters in her district. People listened to and liked what the young attorney had to say.

In spite of all her efforts, Barbara Jordan did not win that 1962 election. It was a big disappointment. However, Barbara did not lose her interest in politics. She was not going to disappear. Barbara Jordan continued to make speeches. She met important people. She spoke to the people who made the laws. Her main concern was laws that would help African Americans.

In 1964, Barbara ran again for the Texas House of Representatives. Again, she lost the election. However, she got several thousand more votes than she had in 1962. "Is it worth it to stay in politics?" Barbara wondered. Her family wanted her to settle down and get married. Barbara had other plans.

In 1966, Jordan decided to run for the Texas State Senate. This time she won! Newspapers all over the country carried the photo of her smiling face and the story of her victory. Barbara Jordan was the first African-American woman in the Texas State Senate. Once again, she had made history.

The fame felt good, but there was something much more important. Now Barbara was a senator, an elected official whose job is to help make laws. As a senator, she could meet with the people in her district. She wanted to know what they had to say about their lives. She would listen to their complaints about civil rights, jobs, and any other problems they had. Then she could help to make or change laws to solve these problems.

Senator Jordan began her term in the Texas State Senate in Austin, Texas, in 1967. The Senate was not the world she was used to. It was all male. It was all white. Still, Barbara did not expect special treatment just because she was an African-American woman. "I wanted them to know I was coming to be a senator," she said. "I was not coming carrying the flag and singing 'We Shall Overcome.' I was coming to work." She let the other senators know that they could relax

Barbara's loyal supporters are always with her to celebrate her victories.

Former President Lyndon B. Johnson was one of Barbara's many admirers. Here, he supports her 1972 race for the United States Congress.

and be comfortable around her. Besides, like them, she was a Texan, and proud to be one. In this way, she earned their trust and respect.

In her six years in the Texas State Senate, Barbara wrote several laws. One was the first Texas minimum wage law. It stated that employers had to pay their workers not less than a certain amount of money per hour. This law was meant to help low-paid workers, like housekeepers and farm workers. Another law said that the state could not work with any company that treated people unfairly because of their race. For example, the state could not work with a company that paid white people more than black people to do the same job. Senator Jordan was also responsible for many environmental laws. These were laws that kept the air, water, and soil of Texas cleaner. Barbara Jordan was definitely making changes.

Barbara's work caught the eye of one fellow Texan—President Lyndon B. Johnson. President Johnson invited Barbara to come to Washington, D.C., to give him advice on national civil rights laws.

In 1971, Barbara decided to run for the United States House of Representatives, one of the two bodies of lawmakers in the U.S. Congress. She won that election easily. Barbara Jordan was the congresswoman from the 18th District of Texas. Now she would help to make laws for the whole United States. At last, she was going to Washington, D.C.!

Chapter Five

MILESTONES IN CONGRESS

By the time Barbara was elected to the United States Congress, she had met many important people. Barbara was well known for speaking strongly and honestly about important issues. She had gained the respect of her fellow politicians—whether they agreed with her or not.

One of those people was Lyndon B. Johnson. Johnson was now the former President of the United States, and still a powerful supporter. He had become Barbara's good friend. Johnson admired Barbara. He felt that her important work served "all the people, all the races, all economic groups." Johnson had helped Barbara raise money to pay for her campaign by attending her big fund-raising party. She needed an important person there to impress the guests and show support for her. The *New York Times* ran a photo of their happy embrace.

The Texas State Senate wanted to give Barbara

On June 10, 1972, the state of Texas honored Barbara Jordan by making her "Governor-for-a-Day."

Jordan one last show of appreciation. They decided to make her "Governor-for-a-Day." They named her president pro tempore, or temporary president, of the Senate. The president pro tempore commonly becomes governor for one day when the real governor and lieutenant governor are out of the state.

Barbara invited students from all of the high schools in her old district to come to her Governor-for-a-Day ceremony. Everyone was there to celebrate Barbara's big day, including her father. Benjamin

Jordan was sick with a heart problem, but he definitely did not want to miss that day. He sat on the platform when his daughter was sworn in. Later that evening, however, Ben Jordan fell ill and was taken to the hospital. When Barbara went to visit him there, he gave her a big, proud smile. The next morning, Barbara Jordan's father died. Still, he had lived to see one of her biggest days. Barbara Jordan had become the first African-American woman governor in this country— even if it was only for one day.

In Congress Barbara served on the House Judiciary Committee. This committee held hearings on the famous Watergate scandal.

Being in the U.S. Congress was a new experience for Barbara. In the Texas State Senate, there were thirty-one members. In the United States House of Representatives, there were 435 members! But Congresswoman Jordan did not let anything stop her from doing her job. Just as she had in law school, Barbara spent a great deal of time reading and studying. That way she could be informed on the issues being discussed in Congress.

In 1973, the first session of her first term, Barbara wrote a **bill**, a proposal for a law, to strengthen civil rights. Her bill stated that any company or school that received money from the federal government had to use the money in a way that was fair to all races. Her bill, known as the Jordan Amendment, was voted in. Barbara had written her first national law! She would soon write many others.

By 1974, other important events were going on in the country. Everybody was talking about the Watergate scandal. Some people who had worked to reelect President Richard M. Nixon in 1972 were accused of cheating. To win the election, they had done things that were unfair and illegal. President Nixon's name became connected to the scandal. There was talk of impeaching him, that is, people wanted to force him out of office by charging him with a crime. Barbara Jordan was on the House Judiciary Committee. This committee had to decide whether to recommend the impeachment. No U. S.

During the Watergate hearings, Barbara expressed her faith in the Constitution in a statement on television. Thousands of people were touched by her words.

president had ever been impeached, tried, and found guilty. It was a very difficult thing to decide.

The committee held hearings to learn more about the situation. During the hearings, one news reporter called Barbara "the best mind on the committee" because she knew so much about the law and was such a powerful speaker. After spending weeks studying the case, each member of the Judiciary Committee made a statement on television to give his or her opinion. Barbara was upset. She did not like the idea of impeaching a U.S. president, but she had read and studied hard. She felt there was only one decision she could make.

On July 25, 1974, Congresswoman Barbara Jordan sat down in front of the television cameras to make her statement. She stated the reasons the Constitution gives for impeachment. Then she stated President Nixon's actions. It was clear, she concluded, that Nixon's actions had gone against the Constitution. "My faith in the Constitution is whole," Barbara said. "It is complete. It is total." Barbara strongly believed that she could not sit by and watch "the destruction of the Constitution." Therefore, she said, she had no choice but to vote for impeachment.

Her words touched people all across the United States. She received thousands of letters. Most praised her, some put her down. Some people thanked her for explaining the Constitution. Once more, Barbara Jordan had made history. The Congress, however, never had a chance to vote on impeachment. President Nixon resigned on August 9, 1974.

After her Watergate speech, Barbara continued to write and support Congressional bills. She paid special attention to those bills that would improve the lives of minority citizens. She listened to the people of Texas and tried to respond to their concerns.

One of Barbara Jordan's most important bills was the extension of the Voting Rights Act. The Voting

Barbara again touched thousands of people with her speech at the 1976 Democratic National Convention. Here, she shares the stage with presidential candidate Jimmy Carter.

Rights Act had been passed into law in 1965. It finally put a stop to the use of poll taxes and tests, which had been used to keep poor people and minorities from voting. Now Barbara wanted to make the law even better. She had heard many complaints from Texans about how Spanish-speaking voters could not read the English ballots. Ballots show the list of people running for office. Barbara decided that the Voting Rights Act should also cover Spanish-speaking people and other minorities. In 1975, she introduced the bill to extend the Voting Rights Act. It soon became law.

In 1976, Barbara received a special honor. She was invited to be one of the two keynote speakers at the 1976 Democratic National Convention. At these conventions, a political party chooses its Presidential candidate. The keynote speakers give important speeches at the convention. On July 12, 1976, Barbara Jordan once again made a speech seen by millions on TV. She was the first African-American keynote speaker at a national party convention. In her stirring speech, Barbara told the crowd of her deep faith in American democracy. She urged them to work to make it even better. Jordan also talked about what the Democratic party stood for through the years. Afterward, she gave her support to Jimmy Carter for President.

The crowd at the convention went wild for Barbara's speech, clapping and cheering and shouting. Some people admired her speech so much that they wanted her to run for vice president. Barbara Jordan, however, had other plans.

STILL MAKING A DIFFERENCE

In the late 1970s, Barbara Jordan began using a cane to help her walk. Later, she needed to use a wheelchair. Nothing, however, could stop Barbara's work.

In 1976, Barbara was elected to Congress for the third time. By now, people all over the country knew who she was. Yet, she felt that she did not want to spend the rest of her life in the United States Congress. She was ready to do something different.

Barbara wanted to share her knowledge so that others could take her place in Congress. She wanted to show other people how they could make changes through the laws, just as she had. With that in mind, Congresswoman Jordan decided not to run for reelection for a fourth term. She officially retired from Congress in 1978.

In 1979, Barbara wrote her life story in a book called *Barbara Jordan: A Self-Portrait*, with co-author Shelby Hearon. That same year, Barbara began teaching

Barbara Jordan is still very much in demand as a public speaker.

at the Lyndon B. Johnson School of Public Affairs at the University of Texas at Austin. Before his death Johnson had told her that he wanted this to be a school for students who had political talent. Barbara was proud to help make his dream happen. When Barbara joined the faculty, so many students wanted to take her course that the dean had to create a lottery system. Only 14 or 15 students were picked to attend each class. There still is always a waiting list. Her students lovingly call her "BJ."

Many people could not believe that Barbara would leave her important job in Congress to teach, but she loves teaching. She feels that nothing is more important than public education because it provides everyone with an equal chance to learn. Barbara enjoys her students because they believe they can make things better through working in the government.

Professor Jordan does not lecture. Instead, she

For her many years of service to her country, Barbara received the Presidential Medal of Freedom from President Bill Clinton on August 8, 1994.

shoots questions at her students to get them to think on their feet. She does not use her course to brag about her own accomplishments. She wants to hear what her students have to say. At the end of every semester, she throws a party for her students at her home. She even plays her guitar, just like old times with the Jordan family! Yes, Barbara Jordan is still having fun.

The former congresswoman receives about a hundred speaking invitations a week, but chooses only about six places a year to make speeches. Her students are the public Professor Jordan most wants to serve right now.

In 1988, an election year, Barbara gave the world a scare. She passed out while swimming and was found floating unconscious in her pool. She was taken to the hospital in critical condition, but in nine days she made a full recovery. "All I know is right now I could not die because this is the Democrats' year, and I have got to be around to celebrate it," Barbara said. Although Republican George Bush was elected to the presidency, Barbara did not let the election or the illness set her back.

Since then, Barbara Jordan has continued to travel and be of service to her country. In 1991, Barbara was appointed as a special advisor to Governor Ann Richards of Texas. She also traveled to South Africa, where she met Nelson Mandela and saw the results of some of her work to fund health care in that country.

In 1993, she received the first Nelson Mandela Award for Health and Human Rights.

In 1992, she was again invited to be one of the keynote speakers for the Democratic National Convention. Everyone was glad to hear that booming voice again! At the end of her speech, the crowd gave Barbara a long standing ovation—they stood up to clap and cheer. Barbara's powerful message helped Bill Clinton, a Democrat, win the election for President of the United States.

One year later, President Clinton appointed Barbara head of the United States Commission on Immigration Reform. This commission helps decide who can come from other countries to live in the United States.

In 1994, President Clinton showed how much he appreciated all of Barbara's hard work by awarding her the Presidential Medal of Freedom. This is the country's highest civilian honor. This is not the only honor Barbara Jordan has received. She has been given over twenty awards and honors worldwide, and she has been awarded over twenty honorary degrees from different colleges and universities!

Today, Barbara's free time is spent visiting with close friends, reading, and keeping up with her favorite sports teams. Barbara likes the Houston Oilers, the Dallas Cowboys, and the University of Texas Longhorns. She especially enjoys the Lady Longhorns, UT's women's basketball team. She shares her home near Austin with longtime friend Nancy Earl.

At an award ceremony in 1993, Barbara told students at Hobart and William Smith Colleges: "Be the highest, the best, the more than more, the excellent. Don't leave anything to chance. Keep pushing."

Barbara Jordan also continues to speak out about the things that matter to her. She urges people to cherish and make use of their opportunities as American citizens. "When you get into that voting booth," she tells them, "you are as powerful and strong as any mighty army." Barbara Jordan's life is certainly proof of that.

Important Dates

1936	Born February 21 in Houston, Texas.
1956	Graduates with honors from Texas Southern University.
1959	Graduates from Boston University Law School.
1960	Begins political career as volunteer for the Kennedy campaign.
1962-1964	Runs for Texas House of Representatives and loses both times.
1966	Runs for Texas State Senate and wins.
1972	Elected to the U.S. House of Representatives from the 18th district of Texas. Named "Governor-for-a-Day" of Texas.
1974	Reelected to Congress. Makes famous Nixon impeachment speech.
1976	Reelected to Congress. Makes keynote speech at Democratic National Convention.
1978	Retires from Congress.
1979	Becomes professor at the University of Texas.
1991	Appointed advisor by Texas Governor Ann Richards.
1992	Makes second keynote speech at Democratic National Convention.
1994	Receives Presidential Medal of Freedom.

Glossary

bill A proposal, or suggestion, for a law. It becomes a law if elected officials vote to approve it.

Congress The branch of national government that makes the laws. The United States Congress has two parts, the Senate and the House of Representatives.

House of Representatives One of the bodies of public officials elected to make the laws. Members are called congresspersons.

Senate One of the bodies of officials elected by the people to make the laws. Members are called senators.

unconstitutional Not permitted by the Constitution, the document which sets forth the highest laws and principles of the United States government.

Bibliography

Blue, Rose, and Corinne J. Nadem. *Barbara Jordan*. New York: Chelsea House, 1992.

Jordan, Barbara, and Shelby Hearon. *Barbara Jordan: A Self-Portrait*. Garden City, New York: Doubleday, 1979.

Haskins, James. *Barbara Jordan*. New York: Dial, 1979.

Weiss, Ann E. *The American Congress*. New York: Julian Messner, 1977.

Index